Strategy Pocketbook:
Building a Strategy for Tomorrow's Organization

MATT D.M. WATSON, Ph.D.

Copyright © 2019 Matt D.M. Watson

All rights reserved.

ISBN: 9781712669945

DEDICATION

To my Brother and chess partner Andy. My first and finest teacher of strategy.

CONTENTS

Chapter 1: Introduction 7

Chapter 2: Current State of Strategy 11

Chapter 2: Phase I Diagnosis 15

Chapter 3: Phase II Forecast 23

Chapter 4: Phase III Ideation 29

Chapter 5: Phase IV: Strategic Testing 35

Chapter 6: Phase V: Transformation 41

Chapter 7: Conclusion 47

Strategy Process 49

References 52

Acknowledgments 55

CHAPTER 1
INTRODUCTION

"Strategy without tactics is the slowest route to victory, tactics without strategy is the noise before defeat."

Sun Tzu

Napoléon Bonaparte wasn't the first General to apply strategies on the battlefield. However, he has been one of the most studied Generals for his mastering of strategic thought. His famous tactic was to divide an army to make it easier to conquer, but his most effective strategy was to build alliances to suffocate his adversaries[1]. Tactics involve knowing what the next move is when it's obvious versus. A strategy is knowing what to do when the path is not obvious. While Napoléon's enemies were playing checkers and toiling in tactics, he was playing chess strategically.

Strategies move an organization down a long-term path, they put the business in a position to take advantage of their competitor, and they theorize on how to achieve greatness. Strategy, like an organization's culture, is harder to define than to understand. Instead of defining strategy, philosophers have offered maxims to understand the subject. For example, if everyone is going in the same direction, then that wouldn't be a strategy, it would be common knowledge.

The dictionary defines strategy as a plan of action or policy designed to achieve a major goal or

---

[1] A. Roberts, Napoleon, A Life

overall aim[2]. The business definition is the plan that dictates where the company will be in the future and a signal indicating where to shift resources. A strategy is a multi-level process of how an entity can determine where they are in comparison to their competitors, where they can take a competitive advantage, and how they can win in the future[3]. Above all, a strategy is the creation of something novel and unique.

No matter how a person defines strategy, it is the heartbeat of the organization. The lifetime of companies continues to shrink due to poor strategies. New ideas and products are followed by cheaper competitors who have improved upon the original design. Successful products in the past would be able to carry a company for decades. Now companies can achieve limited revenue growth before they are squeezed out of the market. This puts the creative tension on a company to continue to innovate and reinvent their strategy. Their only other option is to stagnate and experience a slow death.

---

[2] Merriam-Webster: Creativity
[3] J.L. Gaddis, On Grand Strategy

NOTES:

1. What is my organization's strategy?

   _____
   _____
   _____
   _____

2. What makes your organization unique?

   _____
   _____
   _____
   _____

3. What makes your competitor unique?

   _____
   _____
   _____
   _____

CHAPTER 2
CURRENT STATE OF STRATEGY

"It is not enough to be busy. So are the ants. The question is: What are we busy about?"

Henry David Thoreau

A strategy separates the have from the have nots in the corporate world. Large enterprises can use one of the "Big 5" consulting firms that tap into their industry experts. These exclusive consultants conduct deep research and analysis to determine how the company compares to its competitors. They identify market gaps and provide inside information about the competition's strategy. Taking this data, the consultant can tell the company where to go and how to invest their resources. Unfortunately, the strategy processes have little variation, and all produce similar directions for growth. This results in the fact that the advice that a company receives varies little from the same advice their competitors get. This leads to an unsustainable stalemate in the marketplace.

Smaller organizations run into different strategic issues. The first roadblock is being able to pay for the price of employing a "Big 5" consultant. Next, these organizations struggle to keep up with day-to-day operations. Having a lack of time for the formal strategic process forces small businesses to turn to boutique firms or create a limited strategy by themselves. For that reason, companies then piece together plans on gut feelings and intuitions when they don't have the resources to develop a detailed market analysis. This is the makings of a half-baked strategy.

There are numerous issues that reside in the development of many strategic plans. The first issue is when a company bases its strategic plan on their revenue goals, which is not a strategy but simply a financial plan. Strategies are not on a routine cycle and the outcomes of the annual financial plan are neither strategic nor creative.

A separate issue in the planning process is when the plans are not specific and just aspirational. These plans are then not actively supported or funded. This situation is known as the curse of having too many great ideas that leads the organization to stay in its routine[4].

The third issue with company strategies is that they create a rigid and inflexible plan. Once a company places a significant investment in its strategy, the organization will then struggle if the market conditions change. This leaves the organization in a position where they will be unable to adjust to match the dynamic nature of the market.

---

[4] R.A.W.M. Hollister, Too Many Projects

NOTES:

1. How have you developed your past strategies?

   _____
   _____
   _____
   _____

2. How do your competitors develop their strategies?

   _____
   _____
   _____
   _____

3. What would you have to do to control the share of the market in your industry?

   _____
   _____
   _____
   _____

CHAPTER 3
PHASE I DIAGNOSIS

"Any intelligent fool can make things bigger and more complex. It takes a touch of genius and a lot of courage to move in the opposite direction."

E.F. Schumacher

The process begins with building a strategy team. This doesn't need to be the entire organization, but the team should represent the key parts of the organization. These prominent players not only need to have deep industry insights but also need to influence and move the organization.

The second half of the process is engaging a facilitator to run the strategy journey. They will act as a guide that will manage the process. This helps to enable the strategy team to focus solely on specific tasks and analyses. The facilitator will then piece together the puzzle building the larger picture for the entire organization.

These steps enable the course of understanding the current state of the organization and a diagnosis of the current conditions. This begins with reconfirming what is the value proposition of the organization. What product they provide, who is the customer, what is their value to the customer, and why are they different? Starting with a value proposition that clarifies what value the organization creates for a customer.

A prime example is that of Hewlett Packard (HP), which provides technological solutions to small-to-medium business. This service helps entrepreneurs to efficiently run their business. Unlike technical services from Dell, HP provides dedicated consultants.

These consultants' partner with small companies to provide a free IT service to a capital-limited organization.

Thus, the definition of value is also how the organization plays in the market place. Where does the organization compete in terms of other businesses? Do they sell to consumers or to businesses? If they do sell to businesses, what types of businesses and what do they do with the products?

This leads to the location of the marketplace and where they sell products. Is it a company of consultants that sells at conferences or do they sell tangible products online? Do they have a brick and mortar store, or do they sell both online and in-person? Does the company only sell to distributors or channel partners and don't even interact with the end-users? These are fundamental questions that businesses know and have infrastructures in place to operate in this manner, and it is essential to revisit these topics during strategic sessions as they may provide insights into new routes to market and possible beneficial opportunities.

The next evaluation factor is competition and who are the company's opponents. There are three key competitions. The first being the perfect competition where there are numerous small firms battling for market share but there is not an individual firm that has significant power in the market nor can any firm influence pricing[5]. Modern-day examples would be the restaurant industry where there are too many separate entities to control the market.

The second competitor is the oligopoly where there are a handful of firms that dominate the market. In this model, the firms use their power to increase pricing and maximize profit margins[6]. Modern-day examples would be Home Depot, Lowes, and Ace Hardware in terms of home-improvement shopping.

The last competitor is the monopoly. A modern example of a monopoly is Google and their dominance of internet search where they control 95% of the market. Google dictates then how to set industry pricing[7].

The goal of an organization is to have a blue-ocean monopoly with a revolutionary product that has no equivalent or competition, but this is rare. A red ocean is defined as a product or service where the competition is fierce. Sharks fight over scraps of market share bloodying themselves and create a red ocean. The blue ocean refers to a unique strategy or product where there is no competition, and the waters

---

[5] The Four Types of Market Structures
[6] Defining and Measuring Oligopoly
[7] Monopoly

remain clean and blue[8].

The key elements of evaluating competition are understanding their business in-depth. What they are strong at, where they are weak at, and where are the gaps between what they offer and what their consumers want? If they are a publicly traded company, then their annual reports will provide a level of understanding of what their strategic direction is. Once an organization understands the competition's strategy, they can then attack the new gaps that are opened when they shift directions.

The strategy team will start to understand potential vantage points in the strategy based on the analysis of the competition. The strategy team then bolsters their analysis by factoring in available resources. Resources can be all-encompassing from talented people and capital to assets and natural resources needed for production. Resources influence the strategy by highlighting what is feasible and not. For example, if a potential strategy is to maximize automation development throughout the organization but there is a limitation with being able to hire software developers, then the strategy becomes unrealistic until the resource issue is fixed.

The last evaluation area in organizational

---

[8] W.C. Kim and R. Mauborgne, Blue Ocean Strategy

diagnosis is culture. Culture is a combination of four intersecting areas that define the organization. It begins with the environment where work is completed, the values of the organization, how people are treated, and the overall mission of the organization. The second evaluation area is the operational flow of how work gets completed and how raw materials are transformed and sold to its consumers. The third area is the team dynamic of how the individuals in the organization treat each other, how they work together, and how inclusive are they of each other. Lastly, leadership behaviors are evaluated to understand the organization's decision-making processes and how much control is exerted throughout the organization.

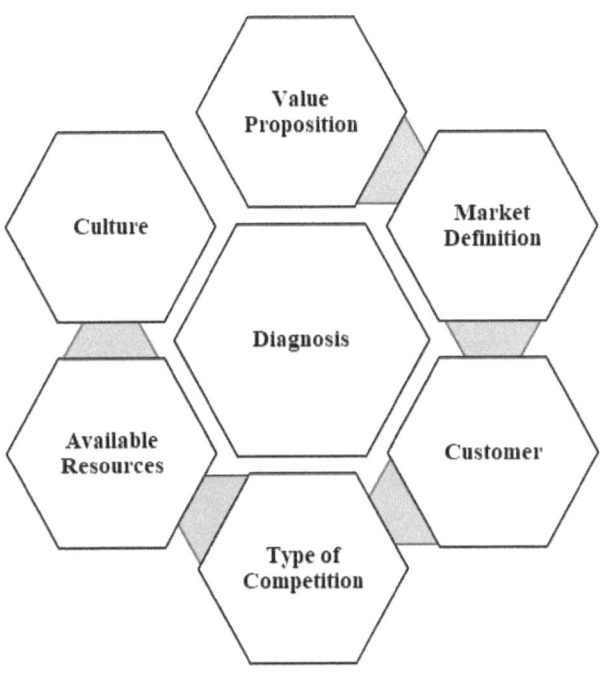

NOTES:

1. How would you define your market?

   _____
   _____
   _____
   _____

2. Who are your customers?

   _____
   _____
   _____
   _____

3. Who are your competitors and why do their customers turn to them?

   _____
   _____
   _____
   _____

CHAPTER 4
PHASE II FORECAST

"The key to making a good forecast is not in limiting yourself to quantitative information."

Nate Silver

The completion of diagnosis moves the team to the second phase which is attempting to predict the future. Futuristic trends highlight the first analysis area in trying to determine what the future will look like. This helps in understand how the world will work in the future[9].

Driving the insight into how consumers will behave, what motivates them, and what they will fear. Fortunately, this unlocks the understanding of what the consumer will want to purchase in the future. This guides the organization's product and how it can morph to match their desires[10]. These insights can be combined with understanding the market trends as to where it has been, where it will be tomorrow, and how to track the position of the company in the future.

The second analysis starts by using Michael Porter's 5 Forces Analysis.

- Starting with the threat of new entrants and how easy it would be to enter the marketplace?
- Second is the analysis of the threat of substitute products. How easy would it be for a competitor to replicate the offering or product?
- The third is the bargaining power of buyers. How easily could consumers drive prices down?

---

[9] L.A.M.M.B. Freedman, Strategy: A History
[10] A Guide to Strategic Planning Environmental Analysis

➤ Fourth is the bargaining power of suppliers. How much leverage do your suppliers have in increasing their prices?

➤ Lastly evaluated is the competitive rivalry and attempting to understand the competition at a micro-level[11].

Now that the organization's competitors are analyzed at a micro-level, the key highlights will begin to self-identify. It will be easier to understand what their strategy is and whether they are moving in the same future direction that other competitors are moving. Other highlights include their positioning in the market and how others compare against them. The result should be an understanding of what makes the competitor special and whether they will have that same unique specialness after making long-term bets on the future.

The final analysis section for forecasting is the understanding of the gaps in the market. If the competition moves in a new direction, then will your organization be able to match their offering head-to-head or will you be able to counter with a new-found weak point? Following the best practices of competitors will make an organization average and the typical market will move in one direction and ignore

---

[11] M. Porter, Competitive Strategy: Techniques for Analyzing Industries and Competitors

another sector. Military tactics and business acumen both point that a war of attrition is started by two opposing forces matching their strengths against one another, while the quickest path to victory is by attacking weaknesses[12]. If a competitor has shifted its strategy, then they have exposed new gaps in the market that can be exploited.

---

[12] J. Keegan, The Mask of Command

NOTES:

1. Are you operating in a buyer or seller market? What event would flip the current state?

   _____
   _____
   _____
   _____

2. What direction is your industry going?

   _____
   _____
   _____
   _____

3. What is your competitor planning to do in the future?

   _____
   _____
   _____
   _____

CHAPTER 5
PHASE III IDEATION

"The reason most people never reach their goals is that they don't define them, or ever seriously consider them as believable or achievable. Winners can tell you where they are going, what they plan to do along the way, and who will be sharing the adventure with them."

Denis Watley

With the insights of self-assessment and competitive analysis, the organization understands the current conditions and their capabilities. It is time to check the makeup of the team. The team can range from an individual to an entire organization but typically more than a few individuals with vast domain experiences are needed to develop a sound strategy. The overarching goal is to employ a nimble team while engaging the entire organization into the process.

The secondary goal would be to build a team that has a very diverse background so that multiple perspectives and ideas are considered. Diverse teams naturally have conflict. They think differently from one another which should cause friction. Friction can be bad for the team if it creates hostility and cliques. However, friction can be great for the team by building team norms that leverage cognitive differences, debates, and candid feedback. Ideally, the facilitator should put the team and leadership through an initial training phase on how to behave and interact with each other during a brainstorming session to ensure that the culture and environment that they create elicits maximum divergent thoughts and opportunities for exploration[13].

---

[13] M. Watson, Common Strategies and Practices Among

The creative brainstorming session can begin once the team is primed for ideation. The brainstorming session can last a few hours, a few days, or even a few weeks. The intent of the process is to generate a range of ideas. The more ideas generated have a direct link to the quality of ideas generated[14]. There are a variety of idea-generating activities that should include potential vertical integrations.

Competent brainstorming also enables the team to determine the potential value nets. A value net as defined in the 1996 book "Co-Opetition" where they designed a model that evaluates potential cooperative partnerships which would make both organizations more competitive[15]. Their model of the strategy was to understand and predict their customers', complementors', suppliers', and competitors' behaviors and strategies. This foresight would then uncover potential opportunities to strategically partner and exploit gaps in the market.

The goal is to have an extended list of potential strategies and variants of original ideas at the end of the workshop. Phase two is to vigorously debate these concepts to fully vet out the merits and flaws of each strategy. A useful activity to enable this debate is to have the participants rank the top strategies. As they

---

Facilitators of Innovative Thinking in Organizations
[14] R. Finke, T. Ward and S. Smith, Creative Cognition
[15] A.A.N.B. Brandenburger, Co-Opetition

try to convince the opposing parties it builds an inclusive process that values challenging arguments over the quick decision-making process.

Another method is to have the team build an evaluation model. This model will factor in cost, risk, and impact against overall payoff in revenue, cost savings, morale, etcetera. The development of the model will provide a quantitative estimate of what are the strongest potential strategies. The crux to the process is for the team to identify a minimum of three strategic options. Then to test these theories over the following weeks.

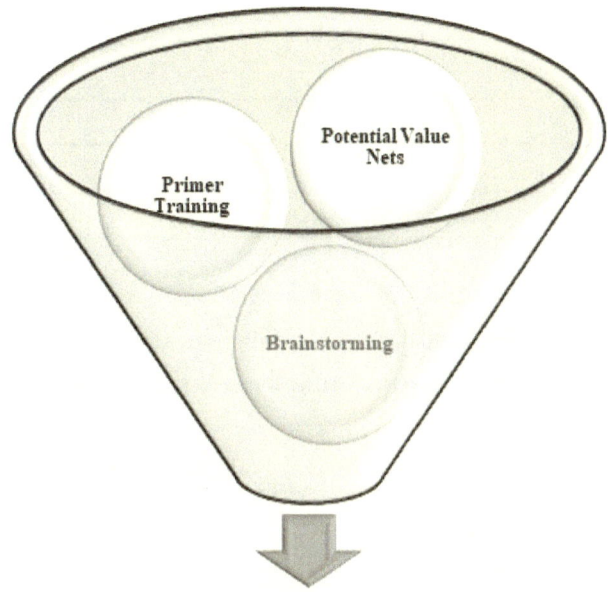

Debating Ideas & Choice Points

NOTES:

1. Can you and your team speak freely with one another during planning sessions?

   _____
   _____
   _____
   _____

2. What would enable debate in your organization during the decision-making process?

   _____
   _____
   _____
   _____

3. Is there a competitor that you could partner with and what would the outcomes be?

   _____
   _____
   _____
   _____

CHAPTER 6
PHASE IV STRATEGIC TESTING

"You can have anything you want. You just can't have everything you want."

Anonymous

Once a collection of strategies has been identified, the intent is to quantifiably test each one. This will determine which strategy will be the winner. The testing process performs risk management to mitigate large strategic gambles. Strategies venture into new, undefined areas where sound data sets do not exist. It is difficult to determine if a strategy will be successful or not with or without data. By strategic testing, this will turn a gamble into a calculated decision.

When designing the test, the first goal is to determine the target customer. This is who will be the target population or user of the experiment. Ideally, the test will be able to segregate that population from other individuals to prevent false data outcomes. Preferably, an organization would want to run the experiments in three conditions of favorable, unfavorable, and most likely economic situations. This would provide insight into the timing as to when to execute the strategy.

This may also lead to identifying what would be the barriers of entry. Being able to identify internal and external factors to entry will provide further insight into the applicability of the strategy. Some barriers may delay or stop a successful entry. Testing prior to full implementation will highlight the barriers before they create major issues. This will also bring forward the unknown unknowns that have derailed numerous strategies. For example, executives had no idea that the release of the new Coca Cola in 1985 would be a disaster. Their new product was met with anger and vitriol by loyal customers that blindsided the leadership team[16]. These experiments may also provide insight into competitive response and how they will react to these organizational feigns.

Moving into the design of experiments, there are several methodologies that can be applied. The key is to design a process that will eliminate bias and provide insight as to whether the strategy would be successful or not. The other factor to be considered is whether the test will be run without interference or if it will model reality where mid-testing adjustments can be made. When running experiments, the focus shifts from performance monitoring to gaining insights and learning outcomes. These insights include the speculation about how the competition will respond, what you would counter with, and what would be their response to the counter.

Lastly, the team will want to perform the CARVER analysis that will then outline the risks and vulnerabilities. Theorists created the CARVER analysis during World War II so that bomber pilots could more effectively drop munitions on enemy targets. Later, this became the threat analysis tool of choice for the Green Beret Special Forces and now more recently for the

---

[16] B. Braiker, New Coke Pops…34 Years Later

business environment[17]. The analysis scores six essential areas consisting of the threat or opportunities' criticality, accessibility, recoverability, vulnerability, eventuality, and recognizability. The analyst weighs the scores to provide a quantifiable insight into strategy selection.

The conclusion is the analysis portion to determine the results and outliers. Were there any anomalies in the testing conditions or was there any market volitivity that would have made a significant impact? Lastly, what changes would be made if these tests were run again? The team will shift to deciding what the key choice points will be once the data has been finalized. In the end, choice points determine which strategy will be selected. If the testing has gone against intuition, then the hope is that the quantifiable data will help sway team opinion and will quickly enable a coalition of aid to support and apply resources.

---

[17] L.A.A.S. Bencie, A 6-Part Tool for Ranking and Assessing Risk

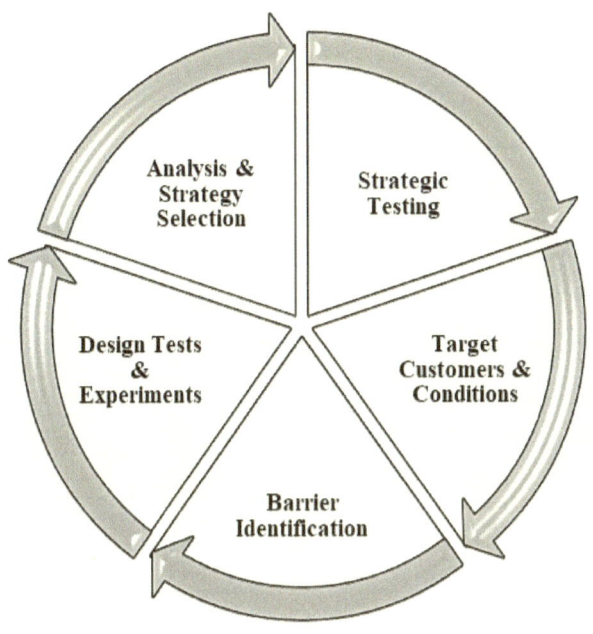

NOTES:

1. What three strategic ideas would you want to see in action?

   _____
   _____
   _____
   _____

2. How would you know if they were effective or not?

   _____
   _____
   _____
   _____

3. What data point would you need to select a strategy to invest in?

   _____
   _____
   _____
   _____

CHAPTER 7
PHASE V TRANSFORMATION

"The result of bad communication is a disconnection between strategy and execution."

Chuck Martin

Once the strategic direction has been identified, the most important factor becomes resource management. Resources will have to shift to support the new direction. The essence of a successful implementation is clarifying what the strategic needs are from each stakeholder. Historically, strategies fail due to not properly staffing the initiatives. Leadership adds strategic goals to overburdened executives which increases their to-do list. Out of necessity, the executives enlist supporters and direct reports who can help them in their spare time. In fairness, these are not truly strategies but tactical initiatives.

A strategic change creates a significant impact on the organization. Performing an impact analysis mitigates collateral damage. Organizational structures will change to support the strategy which will also dedicate full-time resources in making the change successful. Lower priority projects will have to die in order to adequately pay for the new strategy. While the shift may not cost money, it will cost manpower to implement. If manpower stretches thin on numerous projects and priorities, then the true strategy will never come to fruition.

An exercise to help the team conceptualize this change is by running a change-management simulation. It begins with storyboarding the change in strategy and designing the change roadmap. This will help the organization to not only conceptualize the change and what it entails, but it will also identify flashpoints where the strategy can be derailed. Next is to understand the stakeholders of the change and who and how these individuals will be impacted. This provides insight into the risk-management mitigation strategy to help the change go as smoothly as possible.

With this data, the transformation team can initiate their communication planning with the organization followed by the change announcement. This truly kickstarts the changes and the chaos that ensues in the process. Conducting stakeholder feedback sessions will engage team members in change-management planning. Applying a coordinated effort, this will enable greater accuracy in resource allocation, organizational change movement, and strategy adoption.

Last to the strategic process is enabling agility. An organization will want to give the strategy an opportunity to develop and not to overreact quickly. An organization will also want to have tight monitoring of the results to understand what adjustments will be needed to be applied during its implementation. This model resembles that of action research or of Shewhart's Cycle (PDCA: Plan Do Check Act)[18]. This

---

[18] G. Blokdyk, Deming PDCA Cycle A Clear and Concise Reference

will help to refine the understanding of the team as to how success is defined and how score will be kept.

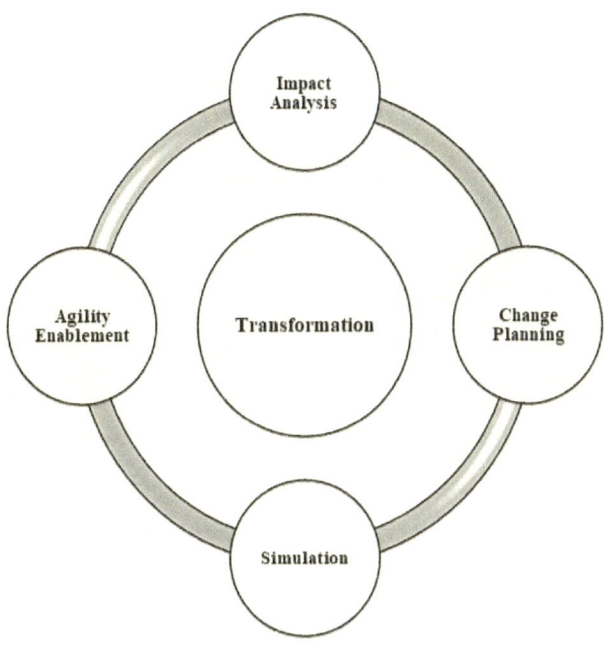

NOTES:

1. What would the impact of implementing a new strategy to the organization?

   _____
   _____
   _____
   _____

2. How could you align your organization to the strategic shift?

   _____
   _____
   _____
   _____

3. Who will oppose this transition and how can you mitigate detractors?

   _____
   _____
   _____
   _____

CHAPTER 8
CONCLUSION

"Strategy is about making choices, trade-offs; it's about deliberately choosing to be different."

Michael Porter

Strategic theorist Roger Martin summarizes his thoughts on a strategy, "If the opposite of your strategy looks stupid, you do not have a strategy." If an organization were to say that their strategy was to become more efficient, the opposite would be that their strategy is to become less efficient. This points to it not being a strategy, but common sense as no organization would strive to become inefficient.

Strategies move an organization down a long-term path, they put the business in a position to take advantage of their competitor, and they theorize on how to achieve greatness. While the finest strategies are the opposite of their competitors, the organization will know that they had the right strategy if eventually, the competition adjusts their strategy to match yours. Then the cycle of innovation does endure.

STRATEGY PROCESS

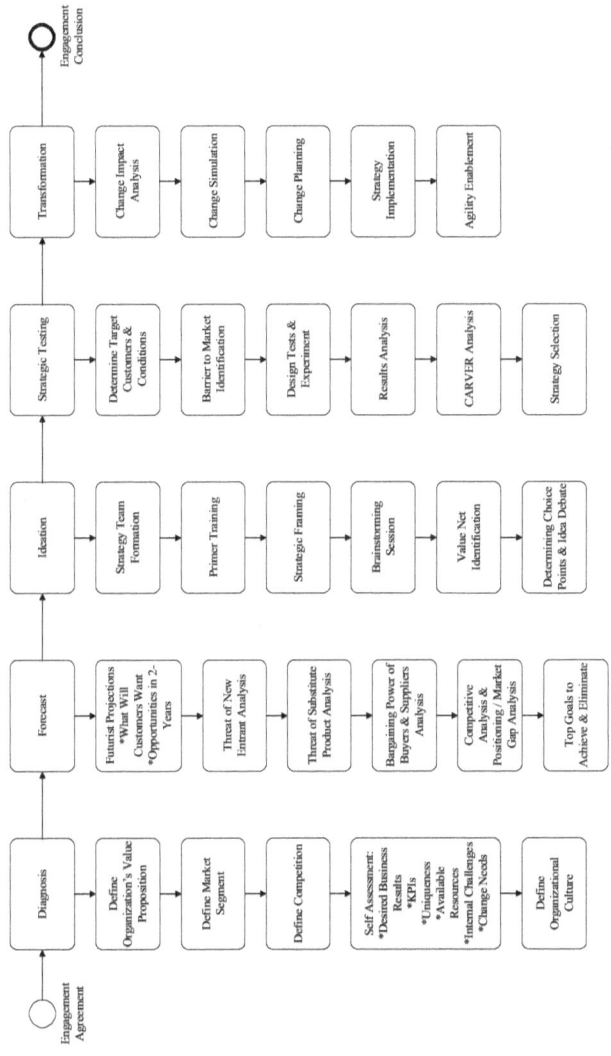

BASIC STRATEGY QUESTIONS:

1. **Diagnosis:**
    A. What is your value proposition?
    B. Define your market?
    C. Who is your customer?
    D. Who are you competing with?
    E. What available resources do you have?
    F. What is your organization's culture?

2. **Forecast:**
    A. What does Porters 5 Force Analysis tell you?
    B. What are the future trends of the industry?
    C. What is you competitor doing in the future?
    D. What gaps will be in the market?
    E. What will the market look like in the future?

3. **Ideation:**
    A. Who should be on my strategy team and how should they interact with one another?
    B. What are potential strategies for moving the organization?
    C. Are there competitors that we could partner with?

4. **Strategic Testing:**
    A. What strategies do we want to test out?
    B. Who are the target customers?
    C. What are the target conditions?
    D. What barriers are in place?
    E. How will you test out these strategies?
    F. What data points do you need to decide?

5. **Transformation:**
    A. What impact will a strategic shift have on the organization?
    B. What does your change management plan consist of?

REFERENCES

[1] A. Roberts, Napoleon: A Life, New York: Penguin Books, 2015.

[2] 07 11 2016. [Online]. Available: http://www.merriam-webster.com/dictionary/creativity.

[3] J. L. Gaddis, On Grand Strategy, New York: Penguin Press, 2018.

[4] R. a. W. M. Hollister, "Too Many Projects," *Harvard Business Review,* 2018.

[5] "The Four Types of Market Structures," 12 April 2019. [Online]. Available: https://quickonomics.com/market-structures/.

[6] "Defining and measuring oligopoly," 12 April 2019. [Online]. Available: https://www.economicsonline.co.uk/Business_economics/Oligopoly.html.

[7] "Monopoly," 12 April 2019. [Online]. Available: http://www.businessdictionary.com/definition/monopoly.html.

[8] W. C. Kim and R. Mauborgne, Blue Ocean Strategy, Boston, MA: Harvard Business Review Press, 2015.

[9] L. a. M. M. B. Freedman, Strategy: A History, Oxford: Oxford University Press, 2013.

[10] "A Guide to Strategic Planning Environmental Analysis," 09 January 2017. [Online]. Available: https://www.captive.com/news/2017/01/09/practical-guide-to-strategic-planning-environmental-analysis.

[11] M. Porter, Competitive Strategy: Techniques for Analyzing Industries and Competitors, New York: Free Press, 1998.

[12] J. Keegan, The Mask of Command, New York: Penguin Books, 1988.

[13] M. Watson, Common Strategies and Practices Among Facilitators of Innovative Thinking in Organizations, Ann Arbor, MI: ProQuest, 2018.

[14] R. Finke, T. Ward and S. Smith,, Creative Cognition, Boston, MA: MIT Press, 1992.

[15] A. a. N. B. Brandenburger, Co-Opetition, New York: Doubleday, 1996.

[16] B. Braiker, "NEW COKE POPS... 34 YEARS LATER," *Adage,* 25 May 2019.

[17] L. a. A. S. Bencie, "A 6-Part Tool for Ranking and Assessing Risk," *Harvard Business Review,* 2018.

[18] G. Blokdyk, Deming PDCA cycle A Clear and Concise Reference, Brisbane: Emereo Pty Ltd, 2018.

ACKNOWLEDGMENTS

My eternal thanks to Kenneth McFarland, Ahli Moore, and Scott Beckett my lifelong mentors. My constant gratitude to my Mother, Barbara Wilson, and Father, Gene Watson who always pushed me to take the long view. A special thanks to my wife Jacqueline and daughters Mia and Josephine. You three have always been incredibly supportive while also being my anchors to pull me back into reality from getting too lost in my work.

9M CONSULTING

About 9m Consulting

9m Consulting helps enable innovation for businesses that are navigating transformation. Unlike other firms, we specialize in building a creative culture that is sustainable versus a one-time event.

Our Approach

9m's approach begins with building the right culture that enables creativity and generates breakthrough ideas. We then take those ideas and help bring them to market. This process starts by diagnosing the current culture so that we can understand what is hindering creative thought and identifying the ideal culture for innovation. We then assist in building and shaping the ideal team dynamic. Following, we put that team through a primer training that maximizes idea generation during a facilitated workshop. We then guide the process of strategy selection and go-to-market planning. Lastly, we assist with ensuring initiative success by helping to align resources and workforce adoption by applying a change management simulation.

Capabilities

9m Consulting is a management consulting firm dedicated to guiding organizations through large scale transitions. Our approach is to work with the client to understand their issues and opportunities. 9m maintains an agnostic philosophy of applying the right solution to the clients need versus a standard one-size fits all solution. 9m's core competency areas are:

- Culture Transformation
- Leadership Development
- Team Dynamics
- Event Facilitation
- Strategic Planning
- Change Management

ABOUT THE AUTHOR

Author and Principal Consultant

Matt D.M. Watson, Ph.D., PMP, is the founder and Principal of 9m, an innovation consulting firm based in Boise, Idaho. He began his career in the United States Air Force as a forward-air-controller, serving in the invasion of Iraq with the 101st Airborne Division. Following Matt's service, he worked with the Bechtel Corporation as an organizational development project manager and training director. Later he worked with Hewlett-Packard as a business strategy project manager and is the Chairman of the Board for the Community Veterans Justice Project.

He obtained his Bachelor of Arts in Organizational Leadership from Chapman University and Master of Arts in Learning Technologies from Pepperdine University. After spending the first half of his career specializing in organizational development, project management, and lean process improvements, Matt focused his craft on the creative and innovation processes while completing his Ph.D. in Global Leadership and Change at Pepperdine University. There he was able to refine his innovation model while completing his research on the enablement of creativity.

He is the author of the following:

- Corporate Musings During the Pandemic
- The Workplace Olympian
- Strategy for the Small Business
- The Strategy Pocketbook: Building a Strategy for Tomorrow's Organization
- Nudge Change Management: Moving Organizations with Data and Transparency
- Rethinking Change Management with Nudges: Transforming Organizations in 45 Minutes
- Facilitating Innovation: Unlocking Moonshots
- Enabling Innovation: Building a Creative Culture in 45 Minutes
- The Leadership That Facilitates Innovation
- From Global Vision to Agile Execution: A Proposed Planning Model
- Simulating the Corporate Reorganization
- Common Strategies and Practices Among Facilitators of Innovative Thinking in Organizations
- Fear and Loathing in the Accountable Culture

www.ingramcontent.com/pod-product-compliance
Lightning Source LLC
Chambersburg PA
CBHW030525220526
45463CB00007B/2717